THE MIRACLE MAN

by James Sprandel

DORRANCE
PUBLISHING CO
EST. 1920
PITTSBURGH, PENNSYLVANIA 15238

Dorrance Publishing Co
585 Alpha Drive
Pittsburgh, PA 15238
Visit our website at *www.dorrancebookstore.com*

ISBN: 978-1-6470-2198-6
eISBN: 978-1-6470-2944-9

THE MIRACLE MAN

ACKNOWLEDGEMENTS

I have to thank God first for allowing me to write this book. He blessed me with the gift of memories. Second is Martha Spiva (AKA Mom). She encouraged me almost every day to add a little bit whenever I thought of something. She was the first person to read my book when I finished.

DEDICATION

This book is dedicated to my mom, Gwendolyn Hemsley Sprandel. Without her love and support, I would not be here today.

THE MIRACLE MAN

I was born to Joseph and Yvonne McCarthy at 12:51 PM on Saturday, September 15, 1973 in Grand Island Nebraska. They named me Joseph McCarthy. My parents were both alcoholics. Me and my older brother, Rick, were raised on the poor side of town.

One morning our mom went to the grocery store and left us at home alone. I was a one-year-old and Rick was three. Our neighbor saw our mom leave without us and she called the police. My dad was at work when me and my brother were picked up by the police. We were taken to Children's Inn in Grand Island.

Not long afterwards, my brother Rick and I were adopted out separately from there. I was interviewed by a few different couples then I met the Sprandels. We talked and they fell in love with me and I was adopted by them. Their names were Roger and Gwendolyn (Gwen) Sprandel.

They changed my name from Joseph Allen McCarthy to James Roger Sprandel.

My new parents were both Christians and my dad was in the Air Force.

I started going to church early and by time I was four years-old it was a routine for me. I was their only child until I was four. That is when for some reason I wanted a younger sister. I got on my knees almost every night for a few months praying to the Lord for them to adopt me a sister.

After a few months, one morning my mom received a phone call from the Children's Inn. They told my her they had a little five-week-old baby girl up for adoption. The next morning my parents and I went to see her. She was so cute. I was the first one to hold her. We adopted her and I named her Christina Grace Sprandel. We called her Tina.

When I was five years-old, me and my dad were going out to eat after church one Sunday morning. I asked him what it meant to be a Christian. Over the next 10 minutes he told me just what it meant. He asked me if I felt like I was ready to become one. I told him yes. He led me to say the prayer and I asked the Lord to come into my heart and soul. I was saved right in front of a Western Sizzlin' Steakhouse.

When I was nine years-old, we were living in Little Rock, Arkansas. One afternoon, me and a friend were practicing soccer in my front yard. My sister, Tina, was watching us practice. My neighbor who was two years older than me came and grabbed her hands and start swinging her around in a circle. He then let her go. She slid on the grass and started crying. I chased him into our backyard and started punching him. His dad came outside and called him. He was crying while he was walking to his dad. Tina, who had watched us fight, came to me and said, "Thank you James."

I said, "Tina, if anybody is going to make you cry, it is going to be *me*." We both laughed. Little did I know that this was the beginning to my rebelliousness.

I used to go to summer camps every year. I have always loved helping and instructing people. I was a born leader. One week when I was 11, I was in a youth camp out of town. I was in my cabin on Friday afternoon by myself praying to the Lord. I then heard a voice like he was standing right behind me. The voice said "James, in your future you are going to have something happen to you that is going to change your life around." I nearly jumped out of my skin! I looked around and said, "Come out. Quit playing." Then I realized I was the only person in the room. I said, "God, if that is you please tell me what's going to happen to me." I heard nothing. The very next day I forgot all about it.

The night before we were heading back home, my roommates and I sat in the middle of our cabin telling ghost stories. At 11:00 PM the staff member assigned to our cabin came in and told us to get to bed. We all stood up and said laughingly, "Heck no, we won't go." He had a towel in his hand which he had wrapped up. He leaned forward and popped me with his towel. I screamed "Ouch." After that, everybody was in their bed.

One hour later, the boy laying in the bed next to me whispered to me "James, I know how to get some whipped cream." We waited till we heard the staff guy snoring before we both stood up. We snuck out of the cabin and went to the kitchen. We went to the refrigerator and there were four containers of whipped cream.

We then went to the guy's car and spread the cream all over the inside of it. We snuck back into the cabin and went to bed. At 6:00 AM we heard a scream. The staff member came walking into our cabin screaming, "Who did this?" We all looked at him and said, "Who did what?" He said, "Who put whipped cream in my car?"

We all looked at each other and started laughing. I said, "We have no idea what you're talking about."

As soon as he walked out of the cabin, we all started laughing. An hour later we were all in the van leaving camp heading home saying, "What an awesome week."

My father was in the Air Force for 26 years which forced us to move around a lot. When I was 13 years-old we moved to Shreveport Louisiana. That was when I started getting into trouble a lot. I started arguing with my parents and at school with my teachers. My life slowly went downhill. I failed eighth grade. I went from making straight A's from kindergarten through seventh grade to making three F's, two D's and one A in 8th grade. I was totally devoted to my girlfriend, friends, and sports. I hardly did any homework. My parents tried to ground me, but I always sneaked out.

In 1988 we moved to Panama City, Florida. In my second year of eighth grade, I went back to making A's again. The teachers were cool and fun. They made us want to learn. That summer of 1988, me and my father built our own house.

I have been hyper all my life. I used to run track, play soccer, football, basketball, volleyball, and do martial arts. I have been competitive all my life. I had to be first at everything I liked to do. One day after football practice, my head coach called me over to him. He asked me if I have ever played center before. I said, "No." He told me that he had coached football for 12 years and I was probably the fastest center he had ever seen. He then asked me if I was going to play football for Rutherford High School next year. Of course, I said, "Yes." He said he could probably have me playing ninth grade varsity.

On November 2, 1988, something happened to me that changed my life around. I was in P.E. that morning and I was running the mile sprint. My fastest mile sprint was a 5:04. I was the county's second fastest mile sprinter, but also I could run short or long distance. I was in the lead till the last quarter mile. At that point, I collapsed. I guess I always been called the class clown, so my coach hollered to me, "Come on James, quit playing." After a few guys passed by me, a friend came over and turned me over on my back. I had passed out. I had blood gushing through my nose and my mouth. Everybody started freaking out. Coach, Miller was jumping up and down pointing at me screaming, "Call 911." The ambulance took me to Bay Medical Center.

The school called my parents at home and told them I had passed out in the middle of the field in back of my school and that an ambulance had taken me to the hospital. They rushed to Bay Medical.

I have never seen my dad cry, but both my parents were crying when they stood by me in the ER.

The doctors discovered that I had experienced a brain aneurysm which means a blood vessel had burst in my brain. I was in ICU for two weeks and then upstairs in the hospital for an additional six weeks as I improved. I had lost the ability to stand, sit up, chew, and even feed myself.

I woke up one morning in the ICU and I could not move my right leg at all. I started screaming for the doctor. He walked in my room and told me to calm down. I told him that I would calm down when I could move my right leg again. It was like my right leg was dead for four days. On the fourth day I could start moving it again. I thanked the Lord for allowing me to move my leg.

One morning I was stuck with an infected IV and less than a day later my right arm was as big as a balloon. My mom told the doctors if they got rid of the swelling, she would not sue them. Two days later it was back to normal.

One morning about 3:30 AM I woke up sweating. I buzzed the nurse and said, "Can you turn the temperature down in my room?" She took my temperature and saw that I was running a 104-degree fever. She quickly pressed the alarm button on the wall. They rolled my bed downstairs and put me in a tub full of ice till my temperature went down.

Then another thing happened. I had an infection in my heart valve. They tried every medicine to get it to go away, but it would not. The doctors told my mom that I would either die or be a vegetable and if I did make it through, I probably would not walk again.

The doctors almost gave up on me but the next morning I had a test, and the infection was gone. I thanked the Lord. A new neurologist came in to check me out and 10 minutes later he said "James, the way it looks, if you make it through this, you might not be able to walk." I thought about it for a minute and then said with a loud tone, "Doc, I think you need to get your monkey ass down to the psycho ward and have your head checked because I know when I make it through this, I will walk again!" My mom busted out laughing. He looked at her and asked, "What's so funny?" My mom said, "Trust me, if he wants it done, he'll get it done." I then told him to get out of my room. He said "But…" and I said, "Get the hell out of my room now." He left. I buzzed the nurse and told her that I did not want him in my room ever again. She said, "Ok, you 'da man."

All my life I've loved dares and challenges. The doctors telling me I would never walk again was like a challenge to me.

On the day before my first brain surgery they had to shave my head completely bald. I got so upset when they turned on the razor, that they had to put me to sleep to shave my head. I woke up an hour later. My mom had bought me a silver balloon and I saw my reflection on it. I looked at the balloon and saw my bald head. I instantly let out a scream. The nurse came running into my room. She asked me where I was feeling pain. My mom who was sitting on the chair beside my bed busted out laughing. She looked at the nurse and said, "He just saw himself bald." The nurse looked at me and said, "If you ever do that again, I will choke you myself."

The next morning, I had brain surgery. I was in the operating room for a few hours. When I came out they brought me into the recovery room and my mom was there waiting for me. My head was still bleeding, and my mom passed out, but my dad caught her before she hit the floor.

An hour later the nurse ran some tests and noticed a blood clot in my brain. I had to go right back into the operating room to get rid of it.

I don't remember that much of me being in the hospital for two months, but I do remember feeling people praying for me. One morning I was in ICU and I was thinking and realized I had put myself first at everything. The Lord was getting sick of being last all the time. I said "Lord, if You allow me to live through this, I will put You first before everything."

After I had everything taken care of in the hospital, I was transferred to the Capitol Rehabilitation Hospital in Tallahassee for three months where I learned to walk, talk, and use my hands has much as I could. The first day I was there I was in a wheelchair. My doctor pushed my wheelchair around introducing me to my therapists. My first physical therapist name was Marcus. He stood right in front of me and said "I am Marcus, your physical therapist. When you are with me, you will be working." Of course, me being the smart aleck I am, I said "Ok, *whatever.*" It turns out he wasn't lying. He made me work all the time. After working with him for two hours a day, five days a week for three months straight, I was walking again.

While I was there, I also made friends with the head nurse, Randy, and the chef. There was a girl from Panama City named Michelle Stump when I was there. She had the same thing I did. She had to have a trachea put in her throat while she was in the hospital, so she could barely talk. We had the same occupational therapy class together. Three days a week we had the same therapist. Michelle was also in a wheelchair. Whenever our therapist wanted us to do something, Michelle would say, "No." That was when I stepped in. I would always bribe Michelle by telling her if she did better than I did, I would buy her a Pepsi. Of course, she agreed. We became best friends while I was there.

I was discharged on a Friday night. Saturday morning, they had a going-away party for me. My therapists and a few of my favorite nurses were there. After the party, my mom and I were walking out the door to leave and I heard Marcus behind me say, "James, come here." I turned around and walked up to him free, with no help. He said "James, you're awesome. You've done what most people can't do." I said to him, "Marcus, you the man." He replied, to me, "No James, you the man. All I did was tell you what to do and you did it by yourself. Keep it up and before you know it you will be running again." We both had tears coming from our eyes. I hugged him and said,

"Thank you very, very, much." I then turned around and got in my mom's car and off we went driving home.

About two hours later we pulled up in my circle. My mom told me to close my eyes. I said "Why?" She told me she had a surprise for me. So, I closed my eyes and we pulled up in the driveway. Keeping my eyes closed, I got out of the car. She then told me to open my eyes. I was in total shock. A bunch of friends from school were standing in front of me. I started crying tears of joy. I gave all the girls hugs and shook all the guy's hands.

About 10 minutes later the Pizza Hut delivery man showed up. I have always loved pizza. Soon after that, I was in the middle of eating a slice of pizza when the TV news van pulled up. I was shocked. The news reporter talked to my parents first and then it was my turn. They showed me giving the girls hugs again and then they asked me a few questions. The last thing I said was, "I would not wish what I had on my worst enemy." I was on the 5:00 PM news that night.

A few weeks later I had to go in for a blood check-up and we got there a little early and my mom asked me if I wanted to go see my favorite nurse. The last time I had seen her was before I went to the rehab center in Tallahassee when I couldn't walk. I said, "Yes." We went into the ICU room and there she was facing the nurse's desk. I loudly said, "Cindy." She froze like a wooden board. She slowly turned around and saw me standing up. Her jaw hit the floor. She ran toward me and planted her lips on mine. I thought I had died and gone to heaven. We then went into the nurse's lounge. I asked her how things were going and who was in my previous room. She told me that a 14-year-old old boy tried to play "chicken" with a car on his bike and had evidently lost and was not improving. He looked just like me, tubes everywhere, the machines beeping every 10 seconds, and his mom sitting in the same chair that my mom used to sit in while I slept. I asked Cindy if I could go see him. She said, "Yes." We walked into his room and I looked at his mom and asked her if I could pray for him. She said, "Yes." As she stood up and walked beside me. I said a prayer for him and then I gave her a brief testimony about what happened to me. I then gave her a hug and walked away.

About two weeks later, my nurse gave me a call and said that the boy had improved and was upstairs getting better. I looked up to God and said "Oh, You da Man."

I started going to the local rehab center for three hours a day—one hour speech, one hour occupational therapy, and one hour physical therapy. One morning nothing was going good for me. My left hand was more spastic than usual. I went to my PT class and sat on the bench. My therapist asked me if I was ready to exercise. I said, "No." I told her that I was having trouble doing everything that day. She sat beside me and said, "James, I've have been a therapist for people it took up to five years to do what you've done in three months." My eyes opened wide open. I said, "Wow, okay let's go."

About one month later Michelle got discharged from the rehab and one Saturday morning Michelle's mom gave us a call. She told my mom that Michelle wanted to talk to me so 10 minutes later we drove to her house. As soon as we walked into her house Michelle grabbed my hand and led me to her room. She closed her door and looked me dead in the eyes. She told me as well as she could, "Thank you James for being there for me when I needed you." She then showed me stuff that she had learned while she was there. We were both crying tears of joy.

A few months later I had to go have an EEG test. After the test I was walking down the hall on my way out when I happened to pass by my neurologist's office. He said, "James, come here please. I need to tell you something." I walked in his office and said "Hi." He then told me that out of all the brain aneurysms: 85% die, 10% are wheelchair or bed ridden and only 5% end up like I am, or better. Has soon as I heard that, I was speechless. I could only do one thing. I looked up and said, "Thank you, Lord."

A few months later I was invited back to the Capitol Rehabilitation for my one-year reunion. Saturday night we went to the reunion. As soon as I through the front door I saw Marcus all the way down the hall. I yelled, "Marcus." He turned and looked at me. I started running towards him. His jaw hit the floor. When I got in front of him he said, "I told you that you would run again!"

I started ninth grade at Rutherford High School, but I did not get along with some of the teachers. The principal of my high school was awesome. One day at lunch the principal, Mr. Spiva, verbally adopted me as his son. The middle of my ninth-grade year I went to a rehab in Ft. Walton Beach Florida. I was there for one month. Then, a representative from a rehab center, named New Medico that was down in South Florida, came to interview me. Three days later my parents and I flew down to South Florida to check the rehab center out. I was admitted.

I was a client there for seven months. We had school on campus, and I held two jobs. While I was there I met a boy named Philip. He was only nine years old and he was learning to walk again just like I had to. One Sunday afternoon I was pushing him in his wheelchair back up to his cabin. I told him "Philip, if you ever need help with anything, let me know. I will be more than happy to help you." The next morning, I was in my PT class when I heard Phillip's therapist in the hallway asking him was he ready to walk. He asked, "Where's James?"

I told my therapist I would be right back. I walked into the hallway and asked Phillip how could I help him. He told his therapist he wanted to walk for me. I asked my therapist if I could give 10 minutes to help Philip walk. She said "Sure." For the next two months, every other day I would walk behind Philip and hold the belt so he would not fall. After being down there for seven months I finally got discharged on a Friday night and I was flying up to Panama City the next morning. I went to Phillip's cabin Friday night to tell him I got discharged that night.

I started to tell him, but he said, "Can I tell you something first James?" I said "Sure." He then said "James, thank you for helping me. I love you." I had tears coming from my eyes. I then told him I got discharged that night. He started to cry. I told him "Philip, I love you too." I then told him that I was going to keep in touch with his counselor to make sure he was walking for his therapist. He promised he would. When I got back to Panama City, Florida a week later I started to call his counselor twice a week. His counselor told me that he was getting better every day. About two months later I called his counselor and asked how Philip was doing. He said, "He's not here anymore." I said "What? What happened? Is he ok?" His counselor started snickering and told me he was discharged two days ago. He then thanked me for helping Philip out. He told me he walked to the car *free* with no help. I cried tears of joy.

When I was 16 and 17 years old, I started arguing with the teachers again. I've never really liked teachers. I've always hated taking orders.

When I was 17, I wrote the Nebraska Children's Home trying to find out about my real family. A few months later I got a letter from them, but it didn't tell me anything I needed to know.

I was in 10th grade at Rutherford again. One day when I was on lunchbreak, Mr. Spiva walked up to me and said, "James, if you think you are about to get in an argument with a teacher or a student, walk out of the class, come see me and I'll take care of it for you." I started to smile. He said with a smile on his face, "Now, don't get into an argument just because you want to come see me now." We both laughed.

In the middle of 10th grade, I switched schools. I started going to Haney Vo Tech school to skip a year. In the mornings I took computer drafting and in the afternoons I took my VE classes. One morning while I was on break, I was walking back into the building and the class bully bumped into me on purpose. I said, "Excuse you."

He looked at me and said, "Who you talking to?" I said, "You." I then went to my class.

Around 12:40 PM I was changing classes when the bully got in front of me and said, "What you got to say now?"

I tried to walk around him and he sucker-punched me in my nose. I screamed, "What the heck are you doing?"

That was when a teacher walked up and told us to go to the Dean's office. I was suspended for three days for fighting. I started to raise my voice to tell the Dean I didn't hit him, he hit me. It didn't work. I was suspended.

A couple months later while my mom was doing her daily exercise run, Tina was on the phone talking to her boyfriend. I grabbed a rag and started popping Tina in the leg. She started laughing and so I kept on. She finally told me to quit, but I popped her one more time. She reached out and scratched my face. I popped her again and that's when she said, "Quit, you crippled bastard." My anger burst out and I hit her in the head. She started crying, threw down the phone and ran into her bedroom.

When my mom got home about 20 minutes later, Tina told her what happened. I stayed in my room the rest of the night. I went to school the next day and my counselor called me into her office. She said my parents didn't want me to live with them anymore. She told me that I was going to be admitted to Rivendell Behavioral Health.

I was there for two months. I got out and moved on the beach into an Independent Living Facility. I had a job while I lived there for two months. I quit my job and I had to move out. My counselor came and picked me up and told me that I was going to Tallahassee to a place there. After being on the road for two hours we pulled up in back of a building. We got out of the car and walked into the building and that was when I realized that it was in a mental hospital. I spent the next two weeks there undergoing medicine testing for my anger spurts and I was there for my 18th birthday.

A couple of days after I turned 18, someone drove me back to Panama City and dropped me off at the City Mission. I stayed the night there and the next day I called my mom and asked her if I could move back with them. She said, "Yes." About a month later I got a letter from the Nebraska Children's Home. They said my biological mom wanted to get a hold of me. They told me to write her a letter and send it to them. I wrote her a letter telling her about my life, my aneurysm and at the end of my story I gave her my phone number.

The middle of December, I was at my friend's house around the corner when my biological mom called my house. My mom answered the phone and when my biological mom asked to speak to me, my mom asked who it was. She said, I am Vonnie, James' birth mom. My mom's jaw hit the floor. My mom told her that I was around the corner at a friend's house and she could go get me. Vonnie told my mom that she would call me back at 7:00 PM.

At the same time something in my mind told me to go home. I walked out of my friend's house and started walking towards my house when I saw my mom jogging down the road toward me. She usually jogged three miles every night, so I thought she was going jogging. When she got right in front of me, she stopped. She then told me that someone had called for me. I then asked her who it was. She said "Guess." I named a view of my friends, but my mom said, "No."

I said, "Who was it?"

She said, "It was your birth mother."

I was speechless. I told her "You better not be joking." She then told me that Vonnie would call me back at 7:00 PM. I was so excited.

Before long, 6:30 PM came around. I was so nervous. At 7:01 PM the phone rang. My sister answered it. She said "James, it's for you." I went in my bedroom and picked up my phone. My heart beat very rapidly. We talked for 15 minutes. I told her about my life and my mom being there for me when I had my aneurysm. She told me that she lived up in Sioux Falls, South Dakota. She told me that I have one sister and six brothers. I went to bed that night the happiest young man in the world.

Two days later I went to the travel agency in the mall and bought a plane ticket up to Sioux Falls, South Dakota.

My mom was sad to see me go, but happy that I would meet my biological family. My plane left Panama City Sunday afternoon at 12:00. It arrived at the airport in Sioux Falls at 8:00 PM. I have never been so nervous in my life. I walked into the airport and there they were–Jerry, Vonnie, Carl, Calvin, and Talawn. I ran up to Vonnie and we hugged. We drove to her house and sat in her recliner side-by-side, talking until three in the morning. I stayed with her for about a month and then I got my own apartment.

I stayed up in Sioux Falls for about two years learning about my biological family. I learned that my real mom had been married quite a few times. I also learned that she was an alcoholic. I met my mom's sister who lived right down the road. I met my sister, Renee when I went to my Aunt Peggy's birthday party. She stayed with me for a week and then went back to Kansas City.

When I met one of my brothers, Jeremiah, he was in Boy's Town, a home for boys. A few months later he and his best friend, Jake, ran away from Boy's Town and came up to Sioux Falls. They stayed with me for a little while. Jake got busted first and was sent back to Boy's Town. Then a week later Jeremiah got busted and was sent back, also.

Vonnie got so sad and upset that Jeremiah was caught, that one morning she took a whole handful of pills swallowed by beer. She called me around 10:00 AM. She told me what she had done. I knew that the pills she took mixed with beer would kill her. She told me that she was getting tired. I told her not to go to sleep. I told her "I'll be right over." As soon as I hung up, I called 911. I told the operator what she had taken with beer and gave her the address to Vonnie's house. I then called a cab and had them take me to the hospital. When I walked in her room the doctor was just leaving. He said, "You must be her son." I answered, "Yes." He then told me that if she would have gone to sleep, she would not have awakened. They pumped her stomach.

A few months later we drove to Grand Island, Nebraska, which was my birthplace, for a family reunion. I finally met my Grandma Buckner. She is one of the sweetest ladies alive and I also found out that I have a huge family..

When I was 19, I contacted my biological father who at the time lived in California. When I was ready to go see him I caught the Greyhound bus from South Dakota to California. When I got off the bus in Ventura, California I saw him standing beside a 1972 Mercedes Benz. He was a big guy. I stayed with him for two weeks and learned a lot about him.

I then went back to South Dakota where I stayed for one more year and then I moved back down to Florida. I rented an apartment on Front Beach Road, but a year later they were raising the rent, so I moved to the other side of the bridge. I rented a one-bedroom apartment.

One afternoon, me and my mom were talking on the phone about my aneurysm. She told me I was lucky I had the aneurysm.

I quickly asked, "How is that lucky?"

She said, "If you would not have had your brain aneurysm, you would probably be dead or in prison for murder."

I said, "Yeah, I guess you're right."

As soon as I hung up I picked up my Bible and asked the Lord to show me a verse that is *my* verse. I closed my eyes and opened my Bible and pointed on the page. I then open my eyes and saw my finger was on Psalms 116:1. I read verses one through nine and almost passed out. It read:

I love the Lord, for he heard my voice; he heard my cry for mercy.
Because he turned his ear to me, I will call on him as long as I live. The cords of death entangled me, the anguish of the grave came over me;
I was overcome by distress and sorrow. Then I called on the name of the Lord: Lord, save me.
The Lord is gracious and righteous; our God is full of compassion.
The Lord protects the unwary; when I was brought low, He saved me.
Return to your rest, my soul, for the Lord has been good to you.
For you, Lord, have delivered me from death, my eyes from tears,
my feet from stumbling, that I may walk before the Lord in the land of the living. (KJV)

I started crying tears of joy. Those verses described my whole life.

About one year later I was in my apartment about to eat dinner when my sister, Renee, called. She wanted me to move to Kansas City to be with her. So, I did. I moved up there on a Thursday.

Two days later my sister and I went to a bar. She was flirting with a Mexican guy when out of nowhere her husband, George, popped up. She had thought he was out of town. They had their drinks and then he came home with us.

As soon as we walked in the house, he grabbed a nine-inch steak knife. He forced me and Renee into my bedroom where I had a couch. Once we were sitting on the couch, George started hitting her in the head with the knife. An hour later she had to go to the bathroom. We all got up and went to the bathroom. When she was finished, we were walking back to my bedroom and George stabbed me in my butt. I screamed. About 3:00 AM we all passed out. I woke up at 7:00 AM by myself and quietly stood up and started walking toward the front door. I was almost there when I heard Renee whisper my name. I stopped and turned around. She asked me where I was going. I told her I was going to her best friend's house to call an ambulance.

She said, "Are you going to call the police?"

I quickly told her "No," then I walked out of the house.

I walked down the sidewalk one block to her friend's house. I rang the doorbell. Her best friend answered the door and told me to come in. I stumbled into her house and laid on her floor and told her what happened earlier. I had her call the police and an ambulance. While I was being taken to the hospital the police arrested George. When I got to the hospital they took an X-ray of my butt and the doctor told me that if the knife had come 1/8 of an inch deeper it would have cut a nerve.

I lived in Kansas City for a little over 12 years. When I was up there, I owned two companies for a few years. I owned C.O.C. Collections and I was a Missouri State Process Server.

In the years I lived in Kansas City, I learned about Renee who I lived with on and off for five years. I found out that she was an alcoholic and would do anything for a beer. While I was living there, I started dating a lady who lived in North Dakota. I ended up moving to be with her there, which made me close my companies. Me and my girlfriend ended up separating after about a year. That's when I got my own apartment.

I lived in North Dakota for about two years. While I was up there I had some medical problems. My first one was Carpal Tunnel Syndrome in my left hand. I had the one of the smartest doctors operate on me. His name was Dr. Kivett. Two weeks later I went back to see him for a check-up. He told me that when he made the incision on my wrist something didn't feel right. He then told me he cut me a little farther and that's when he noticed two aneurysms side-by-side. He fixed my aneurysms and my carpal tunnel. He set an appointment for me to have a full-body CT scan. I found out that I had no more aneurysms.

A couple of months later, I had an appointment to see another doctor in Dr. Kivett's wing. I walked to his nurse and asked her how Dr. Kivett was doing. She said "I don't know. I came to work two weeks ago, and his office was empty." My jaw hit the floor. I asked her if he told anybody he was leaving. She said "No." Automatically I thought that Dr. Kivett was my angel. I thanked the Lord.

Once I got everything handled at the time I moved back down south to Mobile, Alabama because I hate cold weather. I started going to church and Bible studies where I got to know a guy named James. He was an avid skydiver. I've always wanted to go skydiving. One day he gave me the number to the skydiving facility and told me if I made an appointment he would take me there. I did. On June 2, 2012, I went skydiving. I loved it.

While I was in Alabama a bone in my foot started to grow the wrong way. When I stood up my foot hurt extremely bad. I went to three podiatrists and they all told me the same thing. They told me that there was nothing they could do about it. I even went up to Atlanta, Georgia to see a podiatrist that is one of the best. He took X- rays of my foot and told me there was nothing he could do because I have arthritis in my foot. I went home upset.

I was walking up the sidewalk to my apartment when I saw my neighbor. She asked me what was wrong. I told her what the doctor said. She told me to go see Dr. Bose. I told her that I didn't think even he could help me. She told me that he was an awesome doctor. So, I made an appointment to see him. Two weeks later I went to his office and he took X-rays of my foot again. He came into my room and said, "James your foot is flat as a pancake. I'm not going to touch it, but I will refer you to a doctor who has been specializing in your kind of predicament for a long time."

Two weeks later Dr. Bose's assistant called me on the phone. He said they could not get a hold of the doctor. He then said, "Hold on. Let me call you back in a minute." I hung up. About five minutes later he called back. He told me "Dr. Bose is going to operate on you." I was so happy I wanted to scream. A couple weeks later I went in for surgery.

After the surgery I was in the recovery room when the doctor came and told me to not put any weight on my right foot for two weeks. I got a wheelchair from a friend of mine. Two weeks later I went in for a checkup. He told me, "Everything is going good." You can put a little weight on it for two weeks." I was so happy when I went from my second checkup he told me I could walk on it a little bit more each day. A week later I went for my final checkup. Dr. Bose told me that not only did he fix the crooked bone in my foot, but he also created an arch in my foot.

I said, "So I'm no longer flat-footed?" He said, "No."

I almost started crying tears of joy. I told him that he was my angel. He smiled at me and said, "No, I'm just a doctor."

I quickly told him, "I have been to a few different doctors and they all told me I would have to live the rest of my life like this. I can now stand up, jump, and even jog with no pain. You are my angel."

I began going to Planet Fitness and working out for an hour a day, three days a week. I started having a partner to train with. He was a big guy. A couple of days after we were working out together, he asked me what had happened to me. I gave him a brief testimony about my life.

Two weeks later we were in the middle of exercising and he said, "James, can I tell you something." I said, "Sure, what's up?" He then told me that the day before he was at work and things weren't going his way. He was about to give up and then he thought of me. I didn't stop when I had to learn to walk again so why should he give up. An hour later he completed the task. He then said "James, you are my inspiration." I was speechless.

About a month later I walked into the gym and he stopped me and said, "James, you're not going to believe what happened yesterday."

I said, "What?"

He said he was at his job, working with about a dozen guys and they couldn't seem to get the job done so they were starting to give up. He then told them about me. Back to work they went. Two hours later, they finished. He said "James, you're an inspiration to 12 more guys."

I started laughing. All I could say was "Wow, thank You Lord."

I lived in Mobile, Alabama for five years. My mom, Gwen, and I talked once or twice a week. My parents and my Aunt Carol lived in Dothan AL and they were next-door neighbors.

One day something strange happened. When I talked to my dad it was like I was talking to a little boy. He told me he loved his new chair. In conversations with him, I could tell he had dual personalities. Sometimes he talked like a little boy and other times normally.

On the morning of November 29, 2013, my dad walked into my mom's bedroom to check on her.. She was lying in her bed like she was dead. He quickly called 911 for an ambulance. They took her to the hospital and put her in ICU. My dad called my Aunt Eunice in Ft. Walton Beach, Florida and told her that my mom was in the ICU unit. She contacted my Aunt Carol in Dothan and told her. Around 10 o'clock that morning Aunt Carol called me where I lived in Mobile and told me the news.

I called my dad and said, "What happened to my mom?" He said they didn't know yet, but she was in a coma. I told him I would be up there in two hours.

I called a friend of mine and asked him if he could he take me to Dothan to see my mom in the hospital. He said, "Yes." When I got to the hospital about two hours later I walked into her room and saw her laying there with tubes all over her face. I started to cry. She was in a coma that she would never be able to come out of. The respirator machine was breathing for her.

From my conversation with Aunt Carol I realized my dad had been giving my mom some pills to make her muscles wear out. I knew he was responsible, and I told him to leave the room. He did. At that moment, I lost my respect for him and from that time onward referred to him as "Roger" instead of calling him my dad.

I had never seen my mom so thin in my whole life. Even though she was in a coma, I talked to her for about five minutes. I stood beside her bed for about four hours. At 4:30 PM, my dad said he was going to unplug the machine that night. I told him I had to leave. I told him to call me when he does it. He said "Okay."

About 7:20 PM that night my phone rang. It was him. I picked up the phone and I heard him say the two words that I hated to hear him say. "She's gone." I hung up and it felt like my heart had shattered into a million pieces.

I tried to cry that night, but I couldn't do it. I woke up Saturday and started crying for three hours straight. I found out that weekend that as soon as she died, he had her cremated. I called Roger on Monday and asked if they were having a memorial service for her at the church the following Sunday. He said "No, she's in heaven. She's fine where she's at." I hung up and called my Aunt Carol. I told her what he said, and she said, "I'll call you back in a little bit."

About two hours later my phone rang. I picked it up and it was Aunt Carol. She said that she had driven to the pastor's house and asked him about the memorial service. He said, "Yes, they were going to have one on Sunday."

My aunt told me that she wanted me to come there on Thursday but not to let Roger know I'm there until Sunday morning. I promised I would do it. I got to Dothan around 12:00 PM on Thursday. We stayed in her house most the time.

When we went out, because he lived next door, I bent over so that Roger could not see me. Sunday finally came around. Aunt Eunice and my cousin met us at there at the house. We went to church early.

I was looking at the door of the sanctuary when Roger walked in. He looked at me and his jaw dropped. He laid his Bible down about three rows behind us. He started to walk towards me. I clenched my left hand up into a fist. He walked to the row in front of us and stood right in front of me.

I said, "Roger, I have one question to ask you. How the hell can you kill my mom like that?"

He looked directly into my eyes and said, "I don't know James. I'm sorry I don't know."

I told him to leave. When he didn't move I looked at Aunt Carol and told her to get him out of my face. Carol told him to leave and he went back to his seat. About five minutes later church started. The pastor made his announcements and then started speaking about my mom. On the screen they showed pictures of her working in the nursery, where she served regularly in the church. Then he called Roger, Tina, and me up on stage to say a little bit about her.

Roger said his piece first and as soon as he finished, Tina stepped in front of me. She told everybody that she has always been a mommy's girl. My jaw dropped. I looked at my aunts and they are all shaking their head *no*. Everybody knows Tina's a "daddy's girl". After Tina got finished lying I said my piece.

I then walked out of the sanctuary and sat in the lobby area until church ended. When the service ended I walked outside. When Tina came outside, I confronted her. I asked her why she lied in front of the whole congregation. She simply flipped her head to the side and walked off.

When my two aunts came out of the church we went to Ryan's Steakhouse for lunch. Around 1:00 PM my phone rang. It was my friend from Mobile at my aunt's house. I told him we were on the way. We pulled up in her driveway and I went inside her house and got my bag. I walked outside and put my bag in the back seat. I then gave my two aunts a hug and told them I loved them. I went and sat in the car and off we drove down the road.

About a year later I moved back to Panama City, Florida. I had my name on a couple of apartment's waiting lists while I was renting a room in different houses for a little over a year. I happened to be renting a room in a nice big house from a lady who I knew for over 20 years when Hurricane Michael hit our city. I was walking from my bedroom to the kitchen when the hurricane hit my neighborhood. I felt the house shake. I almost peed my pants. (Haha). I looked up and said "Here I come Lord. Here I come."

I thought the house was going to be blown away. Me and my roommates stayed in the kitchen and dining room until the hurricane was finished. We then opened the front door of the house and noticed the front porch was no longer there. We went outside and looked at the house and noticed the second story was no longer there. For the next week and a half, every time I would go outside I got instant depression.

I got ahold of FEMA and they told me that I would have an inspector come check out my room to see how much damage was done. They told me the inspector would be at my house in 2 1/2 weeks. The next day I went to the apartment complex where I was on the waiting list to ask the manager if the hurricane would put bump me back to the end of the list. She told me to go to the FEMA office and get a written letter from them saying that my house was totaled and bring it back to her. I went to the FEMA office and did just what the manager told me to do. I then took the paper back to the manager. She told me that my name was moved up to the top of the list. I said, "Thank You, Lord."

A few days later I caught a plane to Kansas City. I stayed there for two weeks. While I was there, my inspector called me and told me she would meet me at my house on the Saturday when I got back. I got to my house Saturday afternoon and 30 minutes later my inspector showed up. She inspected my room and told me that FEMA would be calling me soon to let me know the amount of money I would be getting from them. I stayed in a room in my landlord's house for two weeks. While I was there, FEMA contacted me and told me how much money I was getting. I had it direct-deposited in my account.

During the two weeks the manager called me and told me to come to her office to fill out some papers for the apartment. I went to the apartment complex office and signed some papers. I was given the key to my future apartment and she told me to go look at it to see if I liked it. I went to my apartment and opened the door. I almost passed out when I walked into my apartment. Two master bedrooms with walk-in closets, a nice size bathroom with a walk-in shower and a nice big kitchen and a nice size living room / dining room. I had tears of joy coming from my eyes. I looked up and said, "Thank you, Lord."

About a week later, I moved in. I had most off my belongings in a storage unit which the hurricane did not hit. It took me a month to get everything up but with the help of a few friends, I got it done. I look back at my life and I can only say one thing.

"Out of all the stuff I've been through in my life, the Lord helped me overcome everything." I pray for everyone who reads this book that they have a new outlook on life, whether they are physically or mentally challenged people and remember, they're people too. "HUMAN LIVES MATTER."

May God bless you.

CPSIA information can be obtained
at www.ICGtesting.com
Printed in the USA
BVHW041610020321
601505BV00004B/57